Mr. Insurance Man

The Financial Services Industry as Seen By an Independent Financial Adviser

by

Bernard J. Denver

authorHOUSE®

AuthorHouse™ UK Ltd.
500 Avebury Boulevard
Central Milton Keynes, MK9 2BE
www.authorhouse.co.uk
Phone: 08001974150

First published by AuthorHouse 6/26/2008

ISBN: 978-1-4343-7873-6 (sc)

Printed in the United States of America
Bloomington, Indiana

This book is printed on acid-free paper.

Mr Insurance Man

THE FINANCIAL SERVICES INDUSTRY
As seen by an Independent Financial Adviser

It began some 40 years ago when bringing up a young family was pretty heavy going from a financial point of view. Being qualified to the level of teaching students from all over the world in the word processing name of Monotype was definitely unfruitful in the financial sense. Waiting for the lucrative lecturer's position of day and evening classes seemed interminable. Yet all around me were successful people bringing up families without the struggle I seemed to be permanently having. Every month along came the insurance man in his posh car. He lived in his own house and his children went to posh schools.

Even though I was in financial distress, I still managed to save a bit for the children with the aid of Mr Insurance Man. Here is the key for the future and it is one I have never let go of. To have some form of life assurance and savings brought about by the advice/service and, above all, the discipline derived from a trusted person close to the family has, is and should always be the guiding light and basic principle of this, our small part in what should be a massive industry.

How many of us today have the complete confidence from our clients to bring us into their world so that we can help them, not just in financial matters but in all matters that help to keep the family life going?

The main purpose of this report is to suggest to you all that before we go any further on a road of whatever you see as the future, let us give some thought of where we were and perhaps a clearer picture of what we should be doing now will emerge.

To continue with my story, I had just over £400 in the world – not bad for the 60's. The £'s were diminishing rapidly so, what to do? The insurance man suggested the purchase of a business in his world of the Co-operative Insurance Society. It sounded like a good idea and so a few weeks later, I parted with my total life savings and "bought a book". I signed the cheque, signed the contract and then the phone rang with my lecturer's position of three full days and two evening classes (£5 per hour in the 60's) – all students fully booked and the opportunity to continue with studies for my degree.

Needless to record the outcome because here I am 40 years later writing what I hope will prove to be some help for others of influence in our world of helping the British people with many problems and, of course, solving them.

"Why on earth do you want to join that bunch of crooks?!" – my father talking and as far as he was concerned he was speaking from experience and not just hearsay. 27 years in the Royal Engineers and never out of the front line during the Second World War had driven some deep penetrating ideals of how to live and survive all types of warfare including crooked insurance salesmen.

And yet here was his son setting out on a new career after wasting every single penny of his life savings on a worthless business. Was he going to follow the example of that fellow who between the wars had sold him a life policy? Of course, the man had said he would get his money back and yet when he was suddenly posted abroad shortly after the First World War (21 years abroad in fact out of 27) and when he wanted his money back – nothing; not a penny was the result. Just a bunch of crooks to tarnish all future contacts with that breed of humans.

A hard life had taught him to keep his mouth shut beyond that one utterance. You never know - something good may come of it. Anyway some of the things he loved most, namely the grandchildren, depended on his son's future success – keep quiet and see what develops.

Well, Dad was right. My first series of income payments came from a percentage of what was collected plus renewals from Motor and General Insurance. The majority of my book's previously recorded income came from Motor and General with Industrial Insurance renewals following on. My first problem was that the income as shown in the book's accounts had mysteriously disappeared – that is apart from £15 which was being paid every two weeks.

My wife cried a lot. At least we could feed ourselves and pay the rent on my previous income. Now we were heading for deep trouble. So, where had the income gone? After an investigation by the manager, it was discovered that the previous owner had transferred to his new book all the worthwhile Motor and General Insurance renewals – a crooked but allowable move as I only actually paid for Industrial and Ordinary Branch (OB) business.

My first serious encounter with the world of business and so far Dad was proving to be correct. I had to do something fast and learning my trade quickly would be the answer. Of course, I would need help and because of my known predicament, the CIS management came to my aid. I soon learnt about all classes of Life and Pension business and I soon learnt that despite being told otherwise, for income reasons, OB suited my way of life and I felt it would lead me to a decent future. I confess to not really understanding how my clients would fare from this direction – that would take more understanding and much learning.

Bicycle clips with the associated bicycle became a way of life. My book in geographical terms consisted of part rural and part outer (very outer) suburbs. I was soon as fit as a fiddle and enjoying the riding - rain, shine and (in those days) snow. It always amazed me how the bicycle moved silently and quickly across lightly laden snow with a few extra sherries from "happy to see you" clients on board.

And so to the serious business of canvassing for new clients, retaining old clients and generally looking after family matters as and when required. Very much as we are supposed to do today really and that is why, if you have had the patience to read this far, you should see where I am heading.

Here I am outside a large detached house knocking on the door hoping to see one of the children who has come of age. I am learning the business under the auspices of the Assistant Manager who repeatedly says it is time to talk about saving for the future. We know a bit about the family, we know the ages of everybody, hence our calling. Much to my surprise, we are issued into a beautiful house, all pleasant and calm. This is not what I expected. I thought we would receive instant resistance to everything about long-term savings, buying a property, having a family and retirement that the Assistant Manager was talking about. No – the family was keen for us to talk to their child and, in any event, so was I – she was gorgeous. Without much ado, she took out a With Profit Savings Plan.

Yes folks, horror of horrors – no transparency, no knowing exactly to the nearest percentage point what the cost was, no knowing what fee or commission the CIS would pay me. However, she did know that I or somebody else would be there to help her through.

She also knew that even if something awful happened tomorrow, her parents would receive monetary help in the form of the life assurance. She also knew that the policy could be used as part of a future mortgage. She also knew that in all probability, it would produce a good return. I could go on about all the good things she was now going to receive.

I learnt very quickly that generally speaking the insurance companies always played fair to clients and their products reflected this fact. For example, if this first client of mine actually kept her With Profit Endowment policy to maturity it <u>actually</u> returned one of the highest of yield factors in the market. Remember this – it does not matter whether transparency is there or not. The one and only thing that matters is that the adviser, the product and the company behind the product put the client first. In other words, transparency with higher costs is far worse than no transparency if as in the past (it is still continuing today) the good companies produced no transparency products like With Profits. How many of us today fully understand the technicalities of our automobiles, yet the results are miraculous compared with just 30 years ago.

At the same time of the above event, the bad companies were coming on board. Could they compete with the good old ones producing first class products for over 100 years? The simple fact was (and once again, still is) no they couldn't, so they cheated and not only cheated, they eventually were actually believed - so much so that they became the voice in regulation. However, that was a long way ahead in our story – and so, back we go.

Our next port of call that same day was a council house once again to see a coming of age young lady. Here we were buoyed up from our previous success and ready with all sorts of useful information.

Well, we got just as far as the doorstep. The father walked by the door just as we were finding out who was who. He asked just one question: "Are you insurance?" "Yes." I replied.

I can remember holding up my briefcase as the first blows hit around my shoulders. Luckily the ones aimed at the head hit the briefcase. The Assistant Manager received a similar number of well-aimed blows. Unfortunately his briefcase was the size of a saddlebag and just as heavy. His briefcase was left on the floor. We retreated backwards down the garden path until our assailant realized his main line of defence, the portcullis (or in this case the front door) was getting just that bit too far away. He ran!

The Assistant Manager looked totally stunned and said, "Well, I'm going back for my briefcase, anyway." I couldn't figure out why he was stunned – completely and utterly shocked, out of it, lost for words – which is literally what happened.

I went home thinking things were quite normal. After all, in a world full of crooks, what else can you expect? Dad, once again, was proven correct. Even so, I most certainly wasn't going to give up now. Surely perseverance with whatever gifts I can offer will eventually win through!

The next day I walked into the office with my usual countenance. I was greeted with a stony silence from everyone. What had I done wrong? In a far corner I spied the Assistant Manager – head down and no acknowledgement coming my way.

"The Manager wants to see you, Mr Denver", said the Manager's Secretary. We were all "misters" in those days. I entered the Manager's office. He was a kindly soul and a great help to me. "Is there anything you want to tell me, Mr Denver?" said he. "No, I don't think so" was my reply.

"Are you sure – are you absolutely sure?" said the kindly soul. "Oh, absolutely." said I.

"Mr Denver, please sit down. I want to talk to you. Last night you and the Assistant Manager were attacked by a man when calling at his property. Isn't that so?"

"Well, yes, that is correct."

"Don't you want to tell me that this job is not for you?"

"No, I never thought of it in that way. You see, being an insurance man would, I was lead to believe, cause a certain type of person to get very angry. So when this bloke thumped us I thought it quite normal." 'Good old Dad had trained me well for such a case,' I was thinking, when interrupted by the Manager with astounding news.

"In all my years of working down the Old Kent Road" (a very rough area in those days) "and the surrounding areas, I was never assaulted. In fact, quite the opposite. I was their friend and confidant. They always wanted to see me."

Well, this was quite a revelation. Perhaps Dad was wrong. Perhaps this job can really help people and perhaps I could become just as well thought of as the Manager.

I didn't know what to say. In fact, I didn't say anything. I walked out of that room in a bemused state. No wonder the office went silent; no wonder the Assistant Manager didn't want to speak. They all thought I would simply go berserk and walk out.

In the six months following that incident, I nearly did walk out on several occasions. Not because the business wasn't being written – it was and I was good at it. The clients were happy – I wasn't. Well, I was getting fed up with all the deaths. The Manager thought I was level pegging at one stage. You know – one new piece of business, one death. It got to six deaths in the first six months and then I stopped counting.

It was only yesterday that I called (as was usual – every two weeks) on a tied cottage to see the lady of the house for the collection of her premiums. The door opened no more than two inches – just enough for me to see one eye and the side of the face of the husband. I had seen him just once before.

It was still a surprise and a mystery when he said, "She's gone, mate." He said these words as he thrust the

IB (Industrial Branch) books at me. All industrial premiums have to be recorded and I thought I would be carrying out my normal duties.

"Gone where – shopping?" says I.

"No – dead." says the old man. "Faithful to you she was, the whole of her life. She was even buried by your lot." By now he had decided to open the door and if you think coal fires are quaint, think again. Those old cottages stank of sulphur and God knows what else. Within seconds my head was in a whirl. Smells, words I couldn't follow and a human who looked like I imagined his Missus did before something awful happened to her.

"It's all there." the old man says, "The books, the policies, the Death Certificate – and I want £460 cash now."

Well, what would *you* say – what would *you* do? I did the same – stood there and sort of smiled. That's what we insurance men do in dire circumstances.

"I'm afraid I don't carry that sort of money. I'll tell you what I'll do though, I'll go back to the office and if all is in order, I'll get you a cheque."

"No cheque mate. We paid you in cash for over 20 years - you pay back in cash."

I leave the house well, loosely speaking, as I never left the doorstep. As I am about to shut the front gate, the old man shouts, "Oi you — don't forget the divi."

"Divi — what's divi?" says I. "You know, stamps — Co-op stamps. She was buried by the Co-op (your lot) and they give stamps. I want stamps."

So there it was. Now I understood what he meant about faithfulness to the Society where she had saved all her life, and now at the end buried by, and the old man wants a discount on his wife's death. You learn a lot about life from things like that. Everything was in order — probate, estate duty — very funny. I returned the same day with the cash.

So, there I am quietly doing my accounts and on answering the phone, a man's voice says his mother has died. After many questions I remember meeting the caller. He is one of two sons living with their mother in the same village as the death already mentioned. I arrange to go along to carry out all the necessary procedures for the death claim.

The day comes and I am dead (excuse me) on time. So I proceed down the street, I notice two other gentlemen walking in front of me. I begin to get suspicious. They have briefcases tucked under their arms, just like mine. They wear coats similar to mine. I can't see their faces, but I bet they look like mine. We all have to cross a road. There is traffic and so we all bunch together, cross the road and, yep, we all turn right.

No! Those dirty rotten brothers couldn't possibly have given us exactly the same time. We all turn up at the front door. The one with the dog collar knocks and both brothers are standing there.

"I can see who you are," says one of them. "Who are you?" he says to the one next to me. "The funeral director" is the reply. Then he says, looking at me, "You are the important one". He physically grabs my collar.

This bloke is big, very big and pulls me in. The other brother shouts at the other two, "You stay there" (outside the house) "You stay there until we know the important bit." You learn a lot about life from things like that.

One death claim did not turn out as I would have liked at all. There were these two lovely old ladies living in a modest house, beautifully kept. It was obviously a house full of love. It became clear that these old ladies were not related in any legal or family way – they nevertheless were blissfully happy. One died and the family of the one that died made sure of their entitlement – no matter what. One heartbroken lady lost everything. Thank God that awful events such as this have largely been stopped with the new Legal Partnership laws.

What must be remembered is that these events still occur, people need help at the time of deep crisis, whether death or financial and often both together.

Over the last few years I have had to deal with death claims now involving millions of pounds per claim. The exact same equation has occurred – in other words I have been asked to help with very long enquiries which would have cost thousands of pounds if I were to charge by the hour.

Believe me, people (our clients) look to us for help – but not in the same way as a solicitor or an accountant. If it wasn't for the fair way/ fair pay of the commission system, I couldn't have helped. More about that subject later. In the meantime I will give you some examples of what I mean.

A friend and client died a few years ago leaving a substantial estate to his wife and family. During many conversations about his estate whilst he was alive, there was just one reference to another portfolio with a bank and that was all - it was never mentioned again. On his death, I asked the widow if she knew about any other investments. "Definitely no" was the answer.

However, I felt uneasy about it and pestered the lady until, after much searching, she came across some papers referring to an investment with a bank. What now took place was unbelievable.

The bank denied all knowledge of any investment. Once, twice, three, four, five times – I tried again and again at every divisional headquarters of the bank. All denied any knowledge of any investments. Eventually, almost by luck it now seemed, I found a trace number and followed it through. £500,000 was the figure the estate received. How he kept it secret from wife and family is another story.

A lovely lady and client died leaving an estate of considerable size to a daughter and son. The whole family wasn't poor, however, I knew the family history which involved much hardship to attain their comfortable existence. The remaining family weren't going to give anything away scot-free and after an introduction to a local solicitor when a substantial fee based on the estate was mentioned, I was told, "You do it." Me 'doing it' meant dealing with all IHT/probate problems. Easy peezy with my experience and, although I didn't receive a fee, I did receive masses of new business from a grateful family.

So, who is going to do this type of work in the future if what I am told is correct our great British public are going to be even more on their own and far worse off in every aspect?

Our story continues with me still running a book with the CIS. By now I was realizing this world of IB/OB/Motor and General was just not me. I loved OB and Pensions plus the ancillary subjects associated with such products. However, there were still major lessons to learn.

One day the Manager called me to his office. He handed me a cheque for a few hundred pounds and said it was a maturity cheque and if I were to see the clients in handing it over, the chances were that I would write some more business. I made an appointment to see the clients. The house was nice – detached and in a good area. I was welcomed and asked to sit down and have tea.

The first words were a surprise. "Mr Denver, I expect your boss told you to deliver the cheque in the expectation of some new business. Well, you won't be getting any. As far as we are concerned, that is it for the rest of our lives. We planned well and this cheque represents part of the planning. We asked you in here so that you can understand what this money means to us. 25 years ago" (1947 as this was 1972) "we took out our first mortgage along with other friends who all bought their first houses at the same time we did. All but us had repayment mortgages and each couple has moved, including ourselves over the past 25 years, a few times.

"That cheque means that we have paid our mortgage as planned, not only that we have had a loan from the CIS and that was paid from the policy. It didn't pay out as much as predicted in 1947, however it also covered us both for life cover. We were hoping to go around the world with what you brought – obviously we can't. Even if you came with a cheque for £1 we would be happy because none of our friends have repaid their mortgages. Every time they moved, they changed their mortgage in one form or another. Every time life assurance had to be re-written becoming more and more expensive and, of course, their health had to be good. In other words the ever moving target got harder to hit.

All these words came from a client – a member of the public – true a highly intelligent one and he was absolutely determined to tell me how a good With Profit Endowment can work. That is the key a good With Profit Endowment *did* work and still would be working if the public was treated fairly by people who should have brought about an educational programme of understanding. Even in those days, the demise of the Endowment was being predicted, not because it didn't work as life cover and a savings vehicle, but because nobody could foresee the massive growth in people owning their own homes and therefore the relationship with protection and savings.

The more I learned about Pensions and OB, the more I knew that the direction I had taken was wrong for me. One day as I was carrying out that very boring job of accounts, I picked up the phone. This was not a willy-nilly exercise. I had pre-determined that there would be four calls – one to each of the top With Profit record offices.   If the phone was not answered after the fourth ring, that company was not for me.   I started at the top:

Standard Life - Very polite, no vacancies.

Scottish Widows – Didn't answer after four rings.

Legal & General – Now although not exactly one of the top four, I phoned them because they were local and one of my clients suggested I should. "Yes, old boy, so what are you doing now?"   Long pause when he heard the answer.   "Well, we could send you an application form." "No thanks."   I put the phone down.

Equity & Law – "Yes, we have a vacancy – I'll put you through to the Assistant Manager."   "Cholmondley Lewis here – what's your name; what are you doing?" After my reply the Assistant Manager said, "Ah good - can you come and see me?"   "When?" says I.   "Right now" is the reply.   "I'm doing my accounts."   "Well stop them and come here."

So started the happiest career period of my life.   I had to sell my business – it took several months and luckily I sold it to a lovely family man who is still in the business and a successful IFA.   It appeared that I had applied for an Inspector's job – something I didn't really understand. All I knew was the history of Equity & Law, how their funds worked and how successful those funds were in getting excellent products produced for the public. I didn't understand that an Inspector meant Inspector of Agencies to control quality and quantity of the company's products through those agencies.

This system of control was the only one in existence for what is now termed the Independent Advisory Market. In our world at the time, the distributors of our products were brokers (all classes) accountants, solicitors, building society managers and bank managers. Production was received from those classes of introducers in the order specified. The rest of the industry was serviced by direct sales forces of various hues, for example the one I came from dealing in all classes of business under the Industrial Insurance banner whilst others, the majority of which were new to the industry, were largely Ordinary Branch.

It is very important to recognize the fact that the way Inspectors worked their agencies produced a very close working relationship with the introducing source. This relationship extended to advice on how to run the business, technical updates, the latest news on the industry, innovative new products (yes, we had plenty of those) and in our case we produced a booklet on Estate Duty Planning which was the bible for most solicitors. In addition to these servicing necessities we were asked by certain types of introducers to call on the public. This nearly always meant evening work and, whilst it may seem we were working all hours of the day and night, in fact we were left to organize our lives as we saw fit. The criteria, as already stated, was quality and quantity production. Our working banner was The Client, The Client, The Client first and foremost in all matters.

When regulation started with FIMBRA I thought the information ready to hand throughout the inspectorate system of agencies with all their intimate knowledge would be used. Obviously, all the direct sales companies would be a different matter. Imagine the cost-saving this would have produced. However, my writing (and I guess many others at that time) suggesting such a move proved fruitless. My first visit from a FIMBRA representative only proved my point. The examination conducted and the result thereof only produced what at least half a dozen Inspectors and their respective companies already knew.

So it has continued with each succeeding regime until now. I detect a complete and welcome reversal in the way the FSA is looking at the future. I do believe at last the unwelcome element within our industry, which has largely remained hidden through means of unnecessary changes, will produce a cleaner industry. I also believe that along the route of Regulation from its inception we have lost a lot of good things the British people need. I can be more specific with the following notes:

The system of quality and quantity control of agencies through the insurance companies should be used as the prime mover of Regulation. We now have a much reduced number of insurance companies operating in the UK and, although the system of Inspector control is not the same, the basic knowledge together with all the necessary written requirements of quality and product production is ready to hand, even more so than in my day. We now have computers which can enter into each insurance company's database to see who is producing what. The why is easily followed up by speaking to the Inspector/Consultant or whatever is the colloquial term now used.

In other words the Regulator already has the method of Treating Clients Fairly and Retail Distribution Review to hand. Think of the cost of implementing these so-called new and innovative ideas as is proposed. Of course, the basis of all good business is TCF and RDR and that has been the practice of good elements in our industry for 200 years.

Working from a desk, masses of information is already to hand and thence to a phone call and finally perhaps a visit to the agency itself. Define TCF and put it into any written context and you produce yet another tool for the unwelcome element to continue hiding with. Use what is already known through the insurance companies, which can be extracted by the method indicated, and all is exposed.

Yes, the human element will always throw a curved ball like, for example, the Inspector may have a bias towards an individual or the agency itself, however the documentary evidence in the form of products sold to clients always show up what is happening. This method for sure stops all the forged paperwork which has occurred with each successive regime change since 1987.

The use of the words "forged paperwork" is not written lightly or without personal experience. I had the misfortune on many occasions to witness the masses of unnecessary paperwork being produced in perfect order to secure a sale. It always fitted the bill exactly as regulation required and it always took responsibility away from the point of sale (and therefore the salesperson) to the client.

In other words, "Look governor, everything is exactly as it should be; the client only needs to read the book – it's all there." Unfortunately the client never had a clue. Have you ever read the rubbish in detail that was produced – and still is to a very large degree?

Over recent years there has been a major change in the way each client's records are now being produced, thanks entirely for some straight and honest thought from the Regulator. There is still some way to go before we get down to what we at the point of sale should be doing (and once did) which was to look after our clients needs quite literally from cradle to grave - and by that I mean companies, their employees and individual clients alike.

So – how did we reach the current situation of where our small section of the Financial Services Industry is in today and what has it cost in monetary terms to our clients and what has it cost in product terms and what has it cost in loss of service to the British public?

If I remember correctly, in 1973/4 the government of the day instructed a report on the industry - it was called the Scott Report. The findings were quite clear and helped me, as an Inspector, to formulate what I believed to be right thinking on how the British people need to be looked after in their needs for the future of the industry. In simplistic terms, the report found the industry to be in a good state of repair. Remember, this report was not designed to look at ethics and, of course, my experience of ethics in the industry to that date was not good. "A bunch of crooks" was how my father and many others described it to me and it was not far amiss for a fair percentage of the sales methods then being applied.

The Scott Report found the Industrial Branch doing what was required – providing a cradle to grave doorstep service. Yes, it was costing the clients in the form of charges, however, the service did not just cover the collection of premiums, it covered a multiplicity of advice and help for the family. Most importantly, it produced a savings culture so that when father died or little Johnny reached the age of majority, the money would be there.

There was no worry about the markets, the method of With Profits or cash accumulation – investments assured that. Did the cost justify the means? The answer is self-evident today. It's no use the government moaning about lack of life assurance, lack of savings, etc when the method of doing so has largely been removed from the average working man and woman. What has replaced the man from the Pru or the CIS or the Liverpool Victoria or whatever is unknown to me. I question just how Mr & Mrs Smith handle all their daily problems without financial help. It is quite obvious that the massive debt we now have would be much smaller with the service and advice once available to sections of our community.

The Scott Report covered the differences between Unit Linked products and With Profits - at that time Unit Linked represented a lower percentage of the market than With Profits. It found and recommended that the basis of savings through life assurance and pensions should be With Profits. Yes, of course, investment models used by all fund managers wherever employed relied on markets, however, the general public need only take the risk of using a Unit Linked product once a solid basis of saving was in place.

The careful and systematic destruction of the reputation of With Profits had already started in the 1960's. Thank goodness a prophecy made by the head of one company that With Profits would not exist in 20 years time did not come true. What was true, however, was the fact that new insurance companies could not offer a history of how their investments performed in the then use of With Profit performance tables. How to shoot down those companies and get a foothold on the market turned out to be simple: "Now look here, do you Mr Expert or Mr Smith know the true costs of running With Profits? Do you know how your money is being used? No? Well, now my products are transparent, here are my charges and you can have a choice of investments, etc. Of course, our premiums per mil will be slightly less than anything in the With Profits field. You can't go wrong!"

So began the new goldmine - not for the clients, of course, but for the new companies and their sales people with large slices for the management. Transparency is useless unless it means lower costs. Lower than what? That was the question. If you build in costs which of course are shown and those costs are the same or slightly higher than what would appear to be unknown costs, ie With Profits funds, then Bingo! – you've hit it rich without having any guarantees whatsoever. You just hope (and hope is the right word) that the fund managers will produce enough to give clients the reasonable return you want.

Unfortunately in 1974 the capitalistic world we live in took an unexpected turn. A group of largely Middle Eastern oil men decided to double the price of oil - the net result of which is known to us all, except perhaps one group of people who seem to have been forgotten. As mentioned, the new companies were selling Unit Linked products without any guarantees whatsoever.

The pensions world provided a quick return in the form of money in the pocket for all companies and specifically the self-employed or people of non-pensionable employment contract. It was easy – virtually two sheets of paper, a Direct Debit mandate and two signatures being the only (and I mean *only*) requirements.

The new Unit Linked companies had started selling this product in the 1960's and it just so happened that these policies were starting to vest in 1974. You can imagine the net result. The unfortunate individuals with Unit Linked contracts could retire with virtually no return or delay their retirement.

Look back and see the With Profit returns - no more need be said. There were press articles on the subject and it was on the radio – however, we weren't talking about the large numbers of people in Personal Pensions as is the case today. It was quickly forgotten except that the Unit Linked companies put an emphasis on changing to Cash five years before retirement – the onus on the client, of course.

It is interesting to note that sometime during the late 1980's when I was an IFA, my own accountant asked me to call on two clients with a Unit Linked pension fund which was being used in a major advertising campaign over a defined period as shown in the advert. The 12-month yield on this particular fund was shown in the major advertising campaign as 12.5%.

My clients-to-be showed me that they were in the fund concerned in exactly that same period, however their return was less than 5% and would I please investigate as they couldn't get any sense from the company. I already knew the answer, however documentary proof was required. I never was able to get any. The answer, of course, is if the client had invested by 12 noon on the day in question and had continued to invest the exact same amount over the next 12 months on a monthly basis (pound cost averaging) and then switched to another fund before 12 noon on the expiry of the year, then the client would have received 12.5%. I managed to get out of the company that not one single policyholder had achieved the advertised yield.

I would suggest that 99% of the British people do not want to be involved with investment management. They need to know their money is in as safe a place as possible and that people who know their business are looking after the money. Thank goodness that With Profit funds are still being produced and once again are showing the results they deserve. They only went into decline because of interference by people who couldn't compete with their excellent results and used inappropriate propaganda to achieve the result we have seen until recently.

It's no use using transparency if the net result is less in the pocket of the client. Transparency is a worthless word when used to line the pockets of the companies who claim to be good for the client. It is fair to say that the good companies who put the client first in every matter (which simply means they actually produce the results) are all the old-fashioned With Profits companies.

It is unfortunate that these companies were forced to change, in various degrees, their strategy towards products and therefore their clients because of this inappropriate propaganda. It is unfortunate that the Regulator, up until the last two years, used this propaganda as the basis of its investment recommendations. It would appear that the good is returning, the bad companies have largely disappeared and good (as always) will win in the long run.

The problem is that the British people, largely unbeknownst to themselves, have suffered badly with the loss of excellent products - by design or sheer ignorance I do not know. A few examples need an airing:

1. **Final Salary Schemes**   Ten years ago there were 5 million private sector scheme members and 5 million public scheme members. Today there are still 5 million public scheme members and just 1 million private scheme members.

    The loss of the private scheme membership is nothing to do with markets. It is 100% to do with interference by the authorities. During my working life the basic funding rate costs for an average membership of 15 and an average age of 35 would have required a funding rate of approximately 15% of salary roll. Today, that rate will almost certainly be 34% plus. No extra benefits are available for the membership. All that is available are masses of useless safeguards and guarantees which only produce masses of dead trees.

I have heard it quoted that these safeguards were necessary – look at Maxwell, etc. Total tosh! It was a simple matter to alter Trustees' rules and leave well alone. It is the extra costs to the employer that stopped this excellent product, even to the extent of making an employer throw in the towel for good and nothing else.

2. **Personal Pensions**   I am in the middle of a yoga session – something I carry out twice a day. It is my evening session and I am lying on the bedroom floor with a news bulletin being relayed in the background. The voice mentions something about a new pension which can do everything a person could wish for – a regular Swiss army knife of a pension. It is a government broadcast. I can't believe it. I rush to the kitchen and ask my wife, Mary, to watch out for this particular advert and give me her opinion of what it would mean

to her. Mary confirmed my worst fears. Oh no! A charter for the salesman to produce masses of no-guarantees pension contracts, a charter for transfers galore <u>and</u> government recommended. I envisaged what would happen and, of course it did. And who was to blame? Why – us, of course.

3. **Pure Endowment**   I have made repeated efforts to tell modern insurance company staff, that this is *not* an Endowment contract. It is in fact a pension contract written under Occupational Rules. This contract was superb – it offered a guaranteed basic sum for a given premium over x years with x being a retirement date. It also offered a whole raft of guaranteed annuity rates. Although it may not seem possible that such a contract existed offering a guaranteed minimum growth rate to retirement plus guaranteed annuity rates, it certainly did and it still exists today in hundreds of thousands of policies. The problem is that nobody seems to be trained to understand these contracts and, of course, the insurance companies no longer want to produce any form of guaranteed return. Why not? Well, I was told by unnamed individuals that it was simply the costs. So you can put the blame on that as you see fit.

4.   **Endowments**   This is a life product. The contract is written in the Life Fund and is taxed as such at source.   These products once offered a safe, secure investment with good returns and life cover to boot.   Some companies still offer the product however, once again, through sheer ignorance or by design and certainly false propaganda they are few and far between.

Phone up any insurance company today and mention the word Endowment (or even Pure Endowment) and the retort invariably is, "We don't do Endowments."   Speak to most members of the public and just mention the word Endowment and see what happens.   I once attended a lecture given by a prominent financial journalist who professed to have the full qualifications of an Adviser and I quote, "You can beat me around the head with a With Profit Endowment Contract and I still wouldn't touch one."   This statement only went to prove our educational system within the industry is either lacking in some areas or the journalist has a common problem in believing what is told as gospel and not finding out the true facts himself. This proves that false statements become the truth.

I also attended several lectures given by the then Chief Actuary of Scottish Amicable (no longer with us) Bill Proudfoot. If only that journalist could have attended such lectures he would not be preaching the rubbish I heard.

The word Endowment used to conjure up something good in our lives being the receipt of a lump sum through inheritance, marriage or indeed a full With Profit Endowment life policy. What went wrong has produced a sad loss for the British public which is reflected in less savings and the way we look at life assurance today.

When I entered the industry there were just two types of Endowment: With Profit and, horror of horrors, Non-Profit. A full With Profit Endowment is in fact two elements – decreasing term and investment. It offers a full and complete guaranteed return of the sum assured after x years. Of course it is expensive, however when you are trying to hit an ever moving target in the form of loan (mortgage) combined with all of life's variances, it offers total stability.

Why is a loan an ever-moving target? Simply because on a repayment basis every time an interest rate changes, unless you keep to that change exactly the target date moves. Life itself proves that nothing remains the same. I have no idea how many families, partnerships or just singles remain in the same place with the same loans throughout their lifetimes. I do know that many get to retirement and have to move because the expected becomes the unexpected. One of my first stories illustrated exactly how a FULL With Profit Endowment works.

The Non-Profit Endowment was slandered by all and sundry. Who but an evil salesperson could sell such a product? Although as an Inspector my company never had that product, it did have its uses and they were very important especially to a section of the banking industry.

A full Non-Profit Endowment was still expensive, although not quite in the same league as With Profit. It offered a 100% guarantee of the sum assured. It also offered very high surrender values before maturity. In other words, it was designed for a specialist market where a loan, not necessarily on a property, needed 100% protection with a possibility of early repayment through the surrender value.   Ignorance killed it.

During the 1930's an enterprising life office offered a completely new product. A Unit Linked Endowment. It was not designed to compete with conventional Endowments – it was designed to give life cover plus a possibility of a good return depending entirely on market conditions. In 1974 GRE had such an Endowment and to my utter amazement, the Nationwide Building Society agreed to allow Interest-only Mortgages on this product.   Nobody could believe that a lender would allow an assignment of a non-guaranteed product and so the rot started.

Low-cost Endowments were next.   This product was designed to reduce the cost of a full With Profit Endowment to the approximate level of a repayment loan. This product now contained a full With Profit element which in itself has two elements (DTA/ With Profits) and Term Assurance - either level or decreasing term.   Responsible companies were careful with the variable With Profit element. The percentage of this element within the policy was not allowed to go below what was considered to be a dangerous level. The proof of the pudding is that these policies are still producing maturity values that on 20 and 25 year terms meet what was expected.

They were never intended to reach so-called targets based on surrender values during their lifetime. Nobody predicted the interference by authorities on With Profit Funds and the related reduction in yield imposed in many ways such as a fine. Even after such a battering they still did the job of protecting the family in offering sums assured and the consequent low rates based on a good health record for the main population.

Compare that today with the population taking out term assurances which by dint of variable loan factors throughout a lifetime and total reliance on good health for a reasonable premium, you are looking at a population not saving and paying massively for life insurance.

Look at today and the huge charges for taking out a loan coupled with an unknown number of term assurance policies needed throughout life offering no return and yet nobody seems to ask why this is happening.

The suitability of an Endowment linked to a mortgage was not just a case of underwriting by the insurance company. It was also underwritten by the lender at branch level. There used to be a collective underwriting procedure between the two at branch level. Not everybody was suitable for an Interest-only loan coupled with a full understanding of how an Endowment worked. I can only guess at the percentages involved. My own experience would indicate a level of no more than 30% of loans being linked to a quality Endowment.

Suddenly, and quite unexpectedly as far as I was concerned, it all changed and with that change came the demise of what should still be available for those who can fully appreciate an excellent product.

To illustrate a microcosm of the cancer that beset our industry, I recall being called out one evening to meet a lady of professional standing. She had an Interest-only mortgage with an Endowment. The Endowment was a low-cost unit-linked product covering just herself. She wanted me to have her husband included on the policy. The product was sold by the lender which was now part of a bank which had an insurance company as part of the organization. After many questions it became obvious that she had no idea how the policy worked and it became obvious to me that the inclusion of her husband would be nigh on impossible – he was not in good health. The policy itself consisted of two or three pages of printed material. The contract had a very low premium for the sum assured - it was very near term assurance rates. In other words, to reach the expected (by the client) maturity value would take a miracle.

It soon became clear that the new tie-ups between banks, building societies and insurance companies (even my old employer, a mutual office, had the same misfortune) would produce thousands of these near worthless, apart from the sum assured, pieces of paper.

The Regulator quite rightly took action, the result of which we see today. Unfortunately the insurance companies did not follow through with a discretionary series of actions which should have eliminated the bad Endowments. Instead, the letters sent to our clients were based on mathematics which should only have applied to the contracts with virtually no investment content. They are based on actual values which in the case of a With Profit Endowment means surrender value.

Surrender values on a With Profit contract means it is based on an actuarial calculation and not on the profits added (which cannot be removed) at the calculation date. To add complication upon complication, low-cost Endowments and only low-cost Endowments (not FULL With Profit) still rely in varying degrees (based on With Profit percentages in the contract) to reach the full maturity (target) value on a terminal bonus, which in itself is variable according to market conditions.

It is true to say that Low-cost With Profit Endowments rely heavily on Terminal Bonuses. However, it is also true to say that with all the variable risk factors associated with markets, investment, interest rates and life itself, the end result being the virtual elimination of all Endowments, is a sad loss to the British people.

There are gains to some sectors of humanity and one is expressed in the mostly foreign purchasers of our good With Profit Endowments and another in the actuarial departments' surrender terms.

To add insult to injury, the professional lady mentioned earlier moved house and shortly afterwards I received a solicitor's letter asking me for personal details as I was going to be sued for mis-selling her Endowment. Such is life! So much for the fact- finding of our legal profession. You can imagine the letter our legal eagle and the lady received from me.

If our own creativity is a recognized hallmark of our time on this planet, then the insurance companies and the Regulator have proved to be very successful in creating a whole new tribe of crooks in our populace. It never ceases to amaze me how the thought of money can bring absolute clarity of memory to a conversation in detail which occurred not last week but even five, ten or twenty years ago.

There is just one fact that overrides all memories. The truth has a formidable power of recovery even after a long period of absence.

What's New?

Our industry was renowned for innovation. If it is still there, it's lost on me. The last time I was faced with the future was when I attended the lectures given by Marius Barnard, famous heart surgeon (his brother Christian followed) from South Africa. He "invented" the Critical Illness policy entirely based on his professional work and rates of recovery, etc. Of course, survival rates from heart disease have changed radically over recent years. Nevertheless, this policy with its multitude of extras is a welcome part of our portfolio.

Instead of expansion into the future with new ideas on protection and safe investments for the British people, we are held back on "what ifs" and "buts". This is not the Regulator's fault for without healthy and expanding financial services direct to the populace, there is no need for Regulation in our quarter. It is the *interpretation* of regulation where this major fault lays. Fear from top to bottom is what has brought an abrupt end to innovation and the same applies all the way to me.

Let's look at two examples; mythical or maybe not, I leave it to you:

A.   I am embedded within an insurance company - an actuary who thinks outside the box (Bill Proudfoot comes to mind once again) and I have this great idea – a new contract that will astound the world.   So here it is everybody, great isn't it? Well before we go any further it has to go to legal, then to this or then to that and who decides? Compliance, compliance, compliance, of course – not the Regulator as all the press would have us believe.

B.   The Regulator wants to bring into my world Treating Clients Fairly (TCF) and guess what? - they will be conducting visits to ensure this is going to happen.   The moment the announcement takes place, I am inundated with offers to join this or that group and this will ensure I can continue to look after clients.   If not, by implication, I will be hung, drawn and quartered – well fined and ruined anyway.

I have attended two meetings with the Regulator and the opposite is true - it is help they are offering. They recognize that as true independents we each look after clients our way – that's what independence is supposed to mean. It is our clients who recognize our true worth and it is our differing ways of looking after them that adds strength not weakness to our status.

As history shows us, to be governed by fear is when reason steps out.

Treating Clients Fairly (TCF) by regulation is probably the most difficult-to-define target ever envisaged by any group of humans. For example, the way I have treated an estate after the death of a client can be seen to be fair by the recipient and the legal advisers. However, other interested parties and their legal advisers may differ in my view. This situation can and does happen simply because pension funds have nomination letters addressed to the Trustees which can be interpreted one way or another and then to top that there could be a Deed of Variation from the Executors. If I have done my job properly, my intimate knowledge of the family, and the effect of the death, will ensure (in my opinion) that what is fair will occur. However, it is my opinion that the outcome is fair and seen to be fair. A Solomon's judgement may not seem to be fair in other quarters, however, to even begin to regulate such matters is beyond my imagination.

To repeat to a certain degree on what has already been said, the Regulator is starting the process of TCF at the wrong end. The creation of our work is labelled, finished and neatly tied up in computer records at the source and completion of our endeavours within the providers.

Leaving aside such matters as the estate issue mentioned above, the mechanics of TCF could be conducted in the following manner:

We, the people at the forefront of meeting the public, no longer have 120 producers of our tools - there are probably between 20 to 50 producers receiving the majority of our business. This makes for an easier start for TCF regulation. Our own creative efforts can be defined into easily recognizable slots by entering into any producer's mainframe.

In other words, without the massive expense of calling on individual companies (both large and small) records of all our efforts are readily available by using modern technology. This creates a level playing field of regulation - no longer will the big boys be able to use their overwhelming usage of numbers, technology and money to what seems to the Regulator to be its heart's desire. It puts big and small on the same plane – that is to say we know exactly what each individual, whether under a big umbrella or a sole proprietor, is doing.

This method of knowing what is going on in contracts being sold to the public also has many add on facets which should be followed through by the Regulator. Employing a fact-finding method such as this will produce an existing record of how the provider is dealing with its products both to the introducer and, more importantly, the public. It not only shows the start

of the contract and related charges, payments of fees and commission, it also will show the completion of the contract, maturity, deaths, vesting and how the producer dealt with such matters. By following up introductions within the producers, a phone call (everything so far conducted electronically) to the Consultant (once called the Inspector) responsible for the control of the introducer (agent) will elicit a report of how individuals within the introducing company behave towards themselves and, by implication, the target of TCF itself.

Then, and only then, can the Regulator visit with total confidence in the full knowledge of how business is being conducted within the organization and by whom on an individual basis.

Do I hear a cry of, "Back door Regulation. Unfair to us introducers!" Well, to those whom can conceive this as wrong, it must surely be right. This method of fact-finding by the Regulator will produce a triple whammy – it will show how the producer treats the public and it will show how the introducer treats the public and it will show how each treat each other.

Commission versus Fees

Once again, the fear factor is introduced into the advisers' lives. Every week some article is published saying that the Regulator will banish commission and we, the evil people who rely on it, will vanish. The survivors will be the big boys who can afford to switch to fees.

Well, let's get a simple fact out in front. It is only by the standardization of commission throughout the industry that has ever or will ever be seen to Treat Clients Fairly. It creates the level playing field the Regulator so wants – it is fair to all and it doesn't represent a rip off. Could a fee be judged in that way? What is a fair fee? Ask a number of solicitors for a quote on a given issue; ask a number of accountants to quote a fair fee. There is no such thing and I believe the public don't want to pay us fees. I cannot remember there ever being a survey on such a matter – it probably would only produce what the questioner wanted in any event.

As a young Inspector I was taught to forget the cost of commission by the Actuarial Department. It represents just 0.3% of ongoing costs. Here is the answer: whilst we have to show the upfront costs, the setting up costs which make commission look like the big one in actual fact, whilst the amounts shown are accurate, they are just part of the ongoing costs of running the whole producer's machine. I checked just recently to see if the 0.3% overall running charge for commission had changed by writing to the Chief Actuary of our biggest producer and the answer is 0.3%.

Guess what has changed in running costs over the last ten years? Whilst at a meeting with the Regulator recently I was surprised and delighted to hear from the same a statement directed at us, "There is nothing wrong with commission." That is true – you are in control Regulator. Make sure commission is fair, fees can never be regulated. Beware of masses of claims, debts, the VAT, court case after court case and a charter for fees not for us – for the legal profession.

We humans always construct any organization in the form of a pyramid. This construction may only be in the mind's eye, however in that manner it has an existence. To study this organization by pulling out a few bricks for the purposes of any form of regulation changes nothing of any consequence.   Obviously the larger the pyramid the lesser the effect to the point of obscurity of what is actually happening within the organization.

It is a waste of time to climb the pyramid trying to discover what is actually the root cause of its existence whether for good or evil.   By inverting the pyramid and studying the one brick often just one person (or perhaps a small committee at best) the whole edifice is revealed.

Education

Well, where is it? The education within our industry is a total disgraceful mess. It is here above *all* else where the Regulator needs to set out with extreme urgency a strict regime that will ensure for generations to come a standardization of learning which results in equal to degree qualifications in the industry.

Taking on people at 21+ with a degree, which may or may not have some relevance in our industry, demonstrates that the individual can study and be of a certain character, that is for sure. However, we should be producing the same within the industry itself.

We have centres of excellence with such bodies as the CII. The knowledge deposited within these bodies is not broadcast to the right quarters.

I know, let's bring in the fear factor once again. Let's bolt on a new examination requirement for all advisers, one that if they don't pass they cannot conduct their businesses in the same way.

Apart from the obvious human rights issue in the above statement, let's examine what it actually means. Education is a joy (or it should be). It is something we should all want at all times. Why try and remove this basic concept with fear is beyond me.

I am forty years in this business – beyond what is still called normal retirement date. I am still willing to learn in my way – not by being forced away on a fool's exercise that will ruin my business for a limited period - and the same applies to many of us who run small businesses. By issuing such decrees of examination requirements we are not increasing the educational value of our industry, we are decreasing it because people with the necessary experience (the ones who should be training the young people) will simply leave and close down their businesses.

Once again we see the industry looking at the wrong end – a completely new educational entity needs constructing right now.

The system of being indentured to a given company (master) had worked in this country for centuries. It was copied by the world at large and it is responsible for the vastly improved and arguably better educated professionals than us around the world today. I hear of many reasons why we stopped. In any event some enlightened industries in this country have started a system of being indentured once again. We need to do the same starting <u>yesterday</u>.

Everything I have discussed thus far is Yesterday. The Regulator is here for tomorrow and not yesterday. In my view the prime objective to ensure a healthy and TCF or whatever you want industry, is through education.

The answer is to recruit young people at the ages of 16-18. This is not the end of their education – it is the start. Every company within the Financial Services industry over x number of employees *must* take on an indentured number of individuals.

There must be a structured educational system through our colleges throughout the UK with a standardized and regulated number of lecturers provided by the CII and other educational organizations. For every recognized career within our industry there should be a minimum standard of education. A structure once used in many of our industries needs to be employed without delay. For example, there needs to be a minimum period of apprenticeship of four years. This period is directly related not just in educational results for each year but is linked to salaries and cost of training.

The result will be an all-round educated journeyman and journeywoman. The gain will be for our industry and the British public alike.

Mr Insurance Man

"Look! That's Mr Insurance Man." The voice was loud – very loud. So loud in fact it stopped many people that Saturday morning in what was once my local village. For what seemed an eternity to me, I too stopped with my two small children. The finger from the other side of the street was pointing at me.

I recognized the figure attached to the pointed digit. He was one of my clients from the local mental institution. Once a month I called at this establishment to visit a number of patients. I had to go through a set procedure before being allowed to see my clients. Although fearful on my first visit, it soon became an enjoyable visit. I was always welcomed by staff and patients. It became clear that my visit was another helpful (I hope) therapy. The staff always made sure the books and premiums were ready. There was always friendly banter between staff, patients and myself.

I often wonder what happens now with the virtual closure of these establishments and Care in the Community. Does anybody visit the mentally ill to bring just one small vestige of a past life of which Mr Insurance Man played a small part?

So, where to now, Mr Insurance Man?

Addendum

We will all shortly be inundated with such expressions as the following, fondly produced by our Regulator the Financial Services Authority (FSA):

1. Treating Clients (Customers) Fairly (TCF) and for those advisers over a certain age: Teatime Comes Frequently (TCF)

2. Retail Distribution Review (RDR) and for those advisers over a certain age: Really Don't Remember (RDR)

The Financial Services Industry wants to know what to call us. So, what is the debate about? Quite simply – are we clients or customers?

The dictionary says:

The Client Prime description: a person using the professional services of …..

The Customer Prime description: a person who purchases goods from a shop.

Fill in the blank:

I want to be a C.................... to all persons who work in Financial Services.